First published in Great Britain 2021 by C.P. Rees

Bethesda Chapel, Narberth, Pembrokeshire

ISBN: 978-1-914485-05-3

Cover design by Rebecca Tadman

Inside Illustration by Robert Jones

Design by Design Marque

Printed and bound in Great Britain

CLIMB THIS MOUNTAIN

AN ATTEMPTED ASCENT OF THE SERMON ON THE MOUNT

C P REES

To the faithful, long suffering and supportive Church of Bethesda whose kindness over the years God has used to make this little booklet possible and whose light has been like a city on a small hill, but praise God for a light and for this to Him be the glory.

With grateful thanks to Keith and Lynnette for their support to the cause of Bethesda Chapel.

SERMON ON THE MOUNT

Contents

Introduction

The Lord's last command in Matthew 28:19-20 to His Church was to go and make disciples of all nations, teaching them to observe all things He had commanded them to do.

This small booklet is published with this goal in mind, that what the Lord Jesus taught His disciples on the Sermon on the Mount would be more applied into the day-to-day lives that we live, so our Heavenly Father would be more glorified in the world.

This is not an in-depth study of the Sermon on the Mount but rather a blast of a trumpet call once again, not only to believe, but to live the life that Christ wants us to live and gave Himself for.

This Sermon, like all sermons, is better heard than read. Dr Martyn Lloyd-Jones said 'This Sermon is more than the sum of its parts and should be studied as a whole.' So, this booklet takes in the whole discourse of our Lord and Saviour Jesus Christ in six short chapters with a broad-brush stroke. Trusting, that you will hear His voice and call to a true Christian life.

The teaching of the Sermon on the Mount did not only come in word only but with authority! You will be confronted on every page with the marching orders from the King and Saviour, and not with the added teachings of tradition, ritual, or the baggage of 2,000 years of Christian culture. Rather than this, we have before us a blueprint of how Jesus expects life in His Kingdom, under His rule, to be lived out and experienced. This mountain is to be climbed.

The hope is that you will experience the flow, force and freshness of His words by the power of the Holy Spirit. God's word says, *faith comes by hearing the word of Christ*, so prepare yourself. The structure of the chapters in this booklet is founded on the premise of what Jesus Christ taught His disciples, by speaking to them and that God is still speaking to us through the same words through His Son in these last days.

This Sermon was not given as a collection of sayings and compiled by Matthew and certainly not written down by the Lord Jesus. This word is a spoken word 'then He opened His mouth and taught them saying' - Matthew 5:2. Although it is not a long Sermon, it is profound, powerful and totally life changing. Therefore, these studies try to capture the impact of this startling and spiritually shocking account of what life in His kingdom is to be like.

This booklet does not come with the sales pitch 'How to apply The Sermon on the Mount and lead a successful life' which is how one book published on this subject was titled. If you think you are leading this life (which Jesus spells out perfectly) then you not only need to seriously think of writing your own book on the subject, but apply for a psychological test of some sort! In the history of the Church, even for Spirit filled believers, all have fallen short of the glory of God.

This is not a 'how to do book' rather a 'please Lord help me to believe' book. Anyone who studies the Sermon on the Mount with the smallest bit of spiritual life will certainly be crying out 'help, Lord I am undone' which is not a bad thing!

The mountain we face before us morally, ethically and spiritually in these chapters is higher than the natural child of Adam would even think of climbing. However, the Christian is not to be dismayed because in the knowledge of Jesus Christ, who has gone before you and has conquered, He has made a way step-by-step. He has promised to be with and empower all who come to Him, to forgive every mistake and pick you up every time you fall. The Christian is like a mountaineer who, seeing the challenge of an Everest, the beauty of a mountain range, the thrill and experience of the climb yet without the dread that they may never make it, and without the presumption that they can. You will learn the truth of the 'impossible possibility' as you hear again the Lord Jesus calling you to walk higher with Him.

These words of the Lord Jesus are challenging, convicting, correcting and comforting. They are words that point us onward and higher and although we may fail often, His desire for us is for good and not ill. They are words which are spirit and life.

We at Bethesda have studied this portion of Scripture in various ways over the years: verse by verse, paragraph by paragraph, section by section, chapter by chapter, taken a microscopic view and an overview, seeing how it applies in ministry, to Church life and in one's personal walk with God.

These studies have not only grown out of a passion to apply the teachings of the Lord Jesus Christ, but also a conviction of the need once again in the Church to be doers of the Word. Delighting in the beauty, purity and simplicity of the life Jesus desires for His disciples. When you read what Jesus expects, because of His coming into the world, the blood He shed, His spirit He gives, this is the most blessed life on earth.

The teachings found in this Sermon are the most practical concerning moral, ethical, relational and spiritual life of the Christian before God and our brothers and sisters. In knowing, applying and re-learning these passages, it will be a means of shining brighter for the glory of God in a dark world.

It's from a conviction that in the discipleship and shaping of God's people, these chapters are most informative.

Each verse has enough to keep any theologian occupied for years, and the implications and its profoundness can make one feel like a rabbit caught in the headlights and unable to move. Yet, the truths we can understand, each and every verse all too well, the problem has been not so much the difficultly of what Jesus has to say but rather the application of it into our lives.

Read as much as you can on the Sermon on the Mount. Read it often, make it a goal to learn the teachings of the Lord in the Sermon off by heart. It is an address to be listened to 'whoever hears these sayings of mine.'

The main themes have been picked out with startling points which Jesus made and emphasised. I have tried to capture in these pages a movement of thought, while keeping the unity of the address but with application. It is not just some teaching to study, it is in its very nature evangelistic, a proclamation of the good news. Yes, it is impossible to keep but the Christian is not crushed although convicted and challenged. Yet everyone in Jesus Christ lives by faith, believing that those who follow Him are pardoned, forgiven and restored. It is this confidence in Jesus Christ our Lord that makes us turn these pages and learn, believing God is doing something deep in you which is of the highest order. What you learn is going to be relevant and needful for every situation in one's living for God, to His glory.

Amen.

CHAPTER 1

PEOPLE OF THE KINGDOM
Matthew 5:1-12

1 And seeing the multitudes, He went up on a mountain, and when He was seated His disciples came to Him.

2 Then He opened His mouth and taught them, saying:

3 Blessed are the poor in spirit, For theirs is the kingdom of heaven.

4 Blessed are those who mourn, For they shall be comforted.

5 Blessed are the meek, For they shall inherit the earth.

6 Blessed are those who hunger and thirst for righteousness, For they shall be filled.

7 Blessed are the merciful, For they shall obtain mercy.

8 Blessed are the pure in heart, For they shall see God.

9 Blessed are the peacemakers, For they shall be called sons of God.

10 Blessed are those who are persecuted for righteousness' sake, For theirs is the kingdom of heaven.

11 Blessed are you when they revile and persecute you, and say all kinds of evil against you falsely for My sake.

12 Rejoice and be exceedingly glad, for great is your reward in heaven, for so they persecuted the prophets who were before you."

When Jesus Christ came into the world He challenged, turned and shook the world to its moral, ethical and spiritual foundations. The force of His teaching as found here in the Sermon on the Mount is still as life-changing as when He first spoke it. Many refer to it but have never heard its message. It is normally misunderstood by the religious and miss-quoted by the Politician. It's used by some who do not even believe in God to defend some ethical lifestyle or moral agenda. There are many different ideas as to what this Sermon is about. It has been called the 'Christian Manifesto'. John Stott in his commentary gives the title, "Christian Counter Culture" a mandate of how Christians should live, *'do not be like them'*. And this clarion call is for all who hear His voice.

However, many who have picked up the Sermon on the Mount have picked up the wrong end of the stick in doing so. We need to get this right at the beginning, the Sermon on the Mount points us to the Mount of Calvary, it is gospel first and not law. These words of Jesus reveal like no other the greatness of our need to be cleansed of our sins in the blood of Jesus. It is not so much the words of Jesus Christ we look to for comfort but rather the wounds of Christ. Jesus was sent from heaven into this world, *'God so loved the world that he gave his only begotten Son'* and it was ultimately to Calvary, He was given to bring lost souls back to God. In completing His mission here on earth, it was needful for Him *'to be born of a woman made under the law'* and live a perfect life. When the time came for

Him to be made known to the world, Jesus started to preach and teach. This Sermon then is something of a by-product of the mission He came to accomplish. He was to teach and speak about the things of God but His teaching is always pointing to the cross and so with this Sermon which is filled with instruction and practicality, spiritual revelation and evangelistic concern, the direction Jesus points us is to our need of a Calvary and a righteousness which is not our own.

Matthew 5:2 says, *'the Lord Jesus opened His mouth and taught them saying.'* The background to those Jesus was addressing foremost in this Sermon and what Jesus was preaching is found in Matthew 4:17, *'Repent for the kingdom of heaven is at hand,'* calling people to change their minds and lifestyles, to humble themselves and to be sorry for their sin, because the kingdom of God is near. Here Jesus addresses those who have known something of this experience, *'poverty of spirit,'* a mourning for sin, willingness to yield to the Lordship of Christ, a hungering for what they desperately need. This is part of the Christian experience in coming to God. In the person of the Lord Jesus Christ; God has come close to us. He is Immanuel, God with us, the Christ, the King and the anointed of God. The reign of God has come and His kingdom is the kingdom of heaven. Jesus begins with these words *'blessed are the poor in spirit for theirs is the kingdom of heaven.'*

Another preacher, however, began a service with these words for the congregation to repeat, *"I am a devil destroyer, I am a weapon in God's hand, I am living the potential of my dreams, I am good looking!"* The difference between the beginning of that Sermon and this Sermon on the Mount is the difference between heaven and hell! Such claims made by that congregation are everything this sermon is not. For, not the great or the good looking (in their own minds), nor the powerful, but the poor in spirit, theirs is the kingdom of God. Jesus was speaking to those whose hearts have been broken through the conviction of sin and sorrow and whose lives have been lived wrongly. Broken people who came to Him, repented, and Jesus wanted to assure them that those who have nothing but who know their need, there is another kingdom in this world and they belong to it. They are those who have come to the feet of Jesus and who are ready to learn from Him. Jesus says *'blessed are the meek for theirs is the kingdom of God.'* They listened to His every word; they were seeking food that satisfies and were hungry and thirsty for righteousness. There is a progression in these pronouncements which first begins with a desperate realisation which makes us look outside ourselves to seek for food in this life. This will satisfy those who are hungry for a righteousness which they do not possess but desperately need.

We now enter into something of the drama of the moment because Jesus is speaking to:

- those people who came to Him in poverty of spirit – humbled,
- those who know what it is to mourn and weep, who need comfort,
- those who do not have in this world, they have come with nothing but they shall inherit the earth,
- those people who are starving, the spiritually bankrupt,
- those who are desperate for the mercy of God, forgiveness and cleansing of soul and peace of heart.

The hymn writer captures the spirit of these people with these words:-

Nothing in my hands I bring,
Simply to Thy cross I cling;
Naked, come to Thee for dress,
Helpless, look to Thee for grace:
Foul, I to the fountain fly,
Wash me, Saviour, or I die.

Jesus starts not with doctrine but with soul needs and when you come to Jesus you will know your soul needs being met in Him. You may not know about the Bible or the gospel, but you do know your great need. You also know that nothing satisfies in this world and you are looking for something 'other'. This Sermon speaks firstly to the desperate, and one of the main reasons many do not get it (Jesus) is because they do not really know their need and so don't know the joy of *'yours is the kingdom of heaven.'* If you are longing for mercy, cleansing, peace and righteousness, then you need to hear these words, *'in Christ you are blessed and* THESE THINGS ARE YOURS.'

There is something else we need to know and hear, not just to whom Jesus is speaking but what He actually says, and if we were there you would never forget it. What a way to start a sermon! What statements! What a word! Jesus begins with the positive and not the negative and then He hammers this nail nine times into the desperate souls before Him. If you do not get it the 1st time, or 2nd, or 3rd, or 4th, or 5th, or 6th, or 7th, or 8th, or 9th - BLESSED.

Some Bible translations, for example the Good News Bible, translate the word 'blessed' as 'happy'. This may not be the best of translations yet it's better than many translations in the etymology of the word (*makaroi)*. It certainly carries this element of what all people crave for in the world - *happiness:* 'Happiness, happiness the greatest gift that I possess,' so sung a British comedian at one time. The American Bill of Rights begins with 'the pursuit of happiness is the right of every human being.' When Jesus spoke this word, He declares who the happy people really are.

For our learning, the point is that no matter what translation you are reading, the word 'blessed' is to be taken in the objective sense and not the subjective. Therefore, the words blessed, happy and delightful are not dependent upon circumstances or feelings, but rather on the fact that we are blessed of God. The word 'blessed' has a far richer meaning. Someone tried to explain it as *'mental well-being'* or *'wholeness'* which conveys a *'peaceful state'*. Again, the issue with translating the word in these ways is that all this *is subjective*. You may be a Christian but you do not feel very happy or peaceful and you are not well in mind. If this is the case, the last thing you feel is wholesomeness and if the truth be told, like these people at the feet of Jesus, so are you.

What we need to know concerning this word is that this is one of those 'God' words. It's a word which even today is found often in religious literature. What Jesus is doing is not telling them how they are feeling subjectively but rather, declaring to them objectively, the reality of the blessing of God. This word is a declaration of God's blessing and it is not what one feels or even thinks, but fact! Although, when the world sees people as described here, they feel sorry for such creatures. However, God declares they are blessed, even though there is a deep mourning in the godly person and for those who have sorrow for sin and sorrow of repentance. The Christian can know what it is to bewail our manifold sins and wickedness and be in the depths of despair inwardly and emotionally but at the same time objectively be in the position of being blessed.

Jesus who is the very Word of God has something to pronounce on those who had come to Him. Ephesians 1:3 *'Blessed be the God and Father of the Lord Jesus Christ who has blessed us with every spiritual blessing in Christ Jesus.'* This word is the exact opposite to the word that God first spoke to Adam, when sin entered into the world and God came that very day and walked in the garden, giving hope but speaking the cursing: cursed was the ground and cursed was the woman in childbirth. However, the word of the gospel begins with blessing - Luke1.42, when Elizabeth met Mary and said *'Blessed are you among women and blessed is the child you will bear.'* There is no other word given like this with such emphasis in the religions all through history on the face of this earth. In a testimony of a young Iranian Muslim woman who came to Jesus Christ, she said she wanted to find God but she felt God was far away from her and when she picked up the Koran what she read was - cursed are dogs, cursed are Jews, cursed are Christians and cursed are women, it is full of cursing she thought. Then one day someone gave her a Bible and she turned to these verses and read repeatedly, again and again 'Blessed', 'Blessed', 'Blessed', 'Blessed'. Even if you do not feel it, or even see it yet you can know it – the declarative word of God on your life. These words are extremely challenging with a depth that is staggering. These beatitudes contain something of repentance and faith and of the crucified life. They are also a contradiction to the world's thinking. From the opening statements of the Sermon, we are being confronted with the message of the cross where the foolishness of God is wiser than men. If we have ears to hear and eyes to see, even these beatitudes point us to the tree, that confounds the wisdom of this world.

By hearing these words of Jesus on this mountain we are brought to our knees to which we see the cross of Jesus on another mountain. These words slay our pride, expose our wrong thinking and pull down the vein imaginations of this world. In taking these words to heart, we begin to know something of those words of the Apostle Paul *'I have been crucified with Christ.'*

Do you see it? Look at it in the person of Jesus Christ, take Him, we are to follow Him. In this world He was poor yet He was rich, but with the poverty of a mind that was to humble Himself. The lowly in Spirit - no one became so poor even to death on a cross. The one who had no comfort at all was the one who had all power in His hands given to Him. Who has hungered and thirsted more than Jesus? Who is more righteous than Jesus? Who is more merciful and purer in heart? Who is a greater peacemaker? Jesus is a contradiction to the thinking of this world. This is the Sermon that shakes the world and it is the message that challenges the core values of our often worldly lives.

Look at these verses and learn them off by heart and understand them. Note the change from the first four beatitudes which refer to the 'Character' to the last four which refer to the merciful, the pure in heart, the peacemakers and the persecuted. These refer more to the conduct of the disciples of Jesus but the first four refer more to the disposition of the disciples. This is a pattern which is found and worked out in the New Testament letters. First we are taught what we *'are'* and then we are told *'how'* to live as a result. In the study of these beatitudes, another point to grasp is that the person who is a Christian is the one who knows something of each of these beatitudes to some degree. There is an order that is spiritually logical and each of these is like a pearl necklace which the Christian person is to adorn. To just have one of these attributes is not it. Study each of them and think how they flow and fit together.

This is the blessed life of the cross-bearing and Jesus is calling them to a life of suffering (v10-12). To be a disciple is to be persecuted, guaranteed! *'Blessed are you who are persecuted for righteousness' sake.'* Rejoice, because it's not 'if' they do but 'when'. They persecuted the prophets from the time of Abel to Zechariah - from A-Z and you are no different.

(v11) Jesus then tells us more of what form this suffering and opposition will take: It will be in the form of words, insults and falsehoods and speaking all manners of things.

Just because we may not suffer physically does not mean we do not suffer. Insults can be painful. *'If you are reproached for the name of Christ, blessed are you, for the Spirit of glory and of God rests upon you. On their part He is blasphemed, but on your part He is glorified.'*

The Christian life consists of living out the life of the cross in the Spirit and this is the call to discipleship. If you want blessing in your life then come to Christ as these did and this will be said of you: 'Yours is the Kingdom of God.' The person who comes to Christ has a transformation from the values of this world. The people of the Sermon on the Mount are the same people found at Calvary's Mount. It is at Calvary where the poorest, meekest and persecuted are found. Fellowship of the beatitudes is fellowship of the crucified. With Him all is lost and all is found. The kingdom of God is made up of cross-shaped people and those people are the ones who are truly blessed.

CHAPTER 2

SHINE BRIGHT
Matthew 5:13-48

13 "You are the salt of the earth; but if the salt loses its flavour, how shall it be seasoned? It is then good for nothing but to be thrown out and trampled underfoot by men.

14 You are the light of the world. A city that is set on a hill cannot be hidden.

15 Nor do they light a lamp and put it under a basket, but on a lampstand, and it gives light to all *who are* in the house.

16 Let your light so shine before men, that they may see your good works and glorify your Father in heaven.

17 Do not think that I came to destroy the Law or the Prophets. I did not come to destroy but to fulfil.

18 For assuredly, I say to you, till heaven and earth pass away, one jot or one tittle will by no means pass from the law till all is fulfilled.

19 Whoever therefore breaks one of the least of these commandments, and teaches men so, shall be called least in the kingdom of heaven; but whoever does and teaches *them,* he shall be called great in the kingdom of heaven.

20 For I say to you, that unless your righteousness exceeds *the righteousness* of the scribes and Pharisees, you will by no means enter the kingdom of heaven.

21 You have heard that it was said to those of old, 'You shall not murder, and whoever murders will be in danger of the judgment.'

22 But I say to you that whoever is angry with his brother without a cause shall be in danger of the judgment. And whoever says to his brother, 'Raca!' shall be in danger of the council. But whoever says, 'You fool!' shall be in danger of hell fire.

23 Therefore if you bring your gift to the altar, and there remember that your brother has something against you,

24 leave your gift there before the altar, and go your way. First be reconciled to your brother, and then come and offer your gift.

25 Agree with your adversary quickly, while you are on the way with him, lest your adversary deliver you to the judge, the judge hand you over to the officer, and you be thrown into prison.

26 Assuredly, I say to you, you will by no means get out of there till you have paid the last penny.

27 You have heard that it was said to those of old, 'You shall not commit adultery.'

28 But I say to you that whoever looks at a woman to lust for her has already committed adultery with her in his heart.

29 If your right eye causes you to sin, pluck it out and cast *it* from you; for it is more profitable for you that one of your members perish, than for your whole body to be cast into hell.

30 And if your right hand causes you to sin, cut it off and cast *it* from you; for it is more profitable for you that one of your members perish, than for your whole body to be cast into hell.

31 Furthermore it has been said, 'Whoever divorces his wife, let him give her a certificate of divorce.'

32 But I say to you that whoever divorces his wife for any reason except sexual immorality causes her to commit adultery; and whoever marries a woman who is divorced commits adultery.

33 Again you have heard that it was said to those of old, 'You shall not swear falsely, but shall perform your oaths to the Lord.'

34 But I say to you, do not swear at all: neither by heaven, for it is God's throne;

35 nor by the earth, for it is His footstool; nor by Jerusalem, for it is the city of the great King.

36 Nor shall you swear by your head, because you cannot make one hair white or black.

37 But let your 'Yes' be 'Yes,' and your 'No,' 'No.' For whatever is more than these is from the evil one.

38 You have heard that it was said, 'An eye for an eye and a tooth for a tooth.'

39 But I tell you not to resist an evil person. But whoever slaps you on your right cheek, turn the other to him also.

40 If anyone wants to sue you and take away your tunic, let him have *your* cloak also.

41 And whoever compels you to go one mile, go with him two.

42 Give to him who asks you, and from him who wants to borrow from you do not turn away.

43 You have heard that it was said, 'You shall love your neighbour and hate your enemy.'

44 But I say to you, love your enemies, bless those who curse you, do good to those who hate you, and pray for those who spitefully use you and persecute you,

45 that you may be sons of your Father in heaven; for He makes His sun rise on the evil and on the good, and sends rain on the just and on the unjust.

46 For if you love those who love you, what reward have you? Do not even the tax collectors do the same?

47 And if you greet your brethren only, what do you do more *than others?* Do not even the tax collectors do so?

48 Therefore you shall be perfect, just as your Father in heaven is perfect."

A person becomes a Christian by coming in faith to the Lord Jesus, humbly placing themselves at His feet. In Matthew 5:1-2, His disciples came to Him, they heard the call of Jesus to repent in chapter 4 for the *'Kingdom of Heaven is at hand.'* They have known poverty of spirit; they are willing to learn and are meek of heart. They also have known a hungering for what is right and have that blessed purity of new birth, experiencing the mercy and peace of God. In addressing these disciples before Him, Jesus begins by assuring them they are *'blessed.'* Although they can expect a life of persecution and rejection (the life of the cross), anyone who wants to be a disciple of Jesus has to take up their cross.

There is also another step in being a disciple, to which every Christian is called and it's to be like salt and light in the world. The Christian life is to be lived and seen by the world and their presence is to be felt in it. To be a follower of Jesus and not to be a light, in word or deed, is not a follower of Jesus. To lose one's saltiness, so Jesus says, is to be *'good for nothing but to be thrown out and trampled under foot by men'* - Matthew 5:13. Yes, we come to Him to escape the lusts of the world yet we are to be in the world as lights.

These next few verses Matthew 5:13-16 are to be underlined and not ignored because the Christian's presence in the world is vital. There is no place for Christians to remain in the salt cellar or to hide their light under a bushel, (v 16) we are told *'to shine before men.'* Christians are to be seen in work and in society and they are to do good works, Ephesians 2:8-10 *'which God prepared beforehand that we should walk in them.'* Therefore, a life which only caused shame or was lived to self is now to be filled with good works, which can amazingly bring glory to God.

The Lord Jesus spells out what these good works are in the following verses of Matthew chapter 5. They are to do with the law of God. Although we are saved by grace alone, salvation is because of the unmerited favour of God in forgiving us freely of our sins. However, don't think for a moment that Jesus has come to destroy the Law and the Prophets. Jesus explains here what it means to fully keep the law as God intended. In Jesus Christ there has been a fulfilling of the law and even the establishing of the law. In the active obedience of Jesus in heart, mind, deeds, living and dying for sins, in Him God's law is fulfilled (v17).

Keeping the law will not save anyone. It is an impossible ask, *'all have fallen short of the glory of God,' 'the whole world is guilty before Him and every mouth stopped.'* The law of God condemns us but look at this verse, an important verse in understanding Jesus' relationship to the law and our relationship then in Him to it. Jesus did not come to make void the law but to establish it (Romans 3:31). Before we add up 2 and 2 and make 5, Jesus preaches not about the law but about Himself. The good news is all about, not what we are to do, but what Jesus has done. When Jesus was on earth, one of the unique things about His teaching and preaching was that He always pointed to Himself, telling people who He was and what He had come to do and would do for all who believe in Him. Here He makes this great statement that He had not come to destroy the Law or Prophets but to fulfil it, Jesus understood Himself to be the fulfilment of the Scriptures. The Old Testament Scriptures points to Him, His life, His work, His teaching and most of all His death for sin and His resurrection (1 Cor 15:3-4). Therefore, when we read of the law (for example the 10 commandments) we are told these laws are to point us to Jesus. Galatians 3:24; *'Therefore the Law was a tutor to bring us to Christ, that we might be justified by faith.'*

In Jesus Christ the whole law, every last jot and tittle of it, is fulfilled and all the requirements of divine justice. From the understanding of these verses, you begin to have a new relationship with God's law built on faith in Jesus Christ, where in Him all has been met. Jesus is telling them important news about Himself. The law was a big thing in the life of the Jew and they lived every hour and day by it but now they hear that Jesus has fulfilled it. The Amplified version says, *'For truly I tell you, until heaven and earth pass away and perish not even the smallest letter nor one little hook will pass from the law until all things it foreshadows have been accomplished.'*

The Christian is not to break the law of God or to teach others to do so. Jesus said "I *am the light of the world, whoever follows Me shall not walk in darkness but will have the light of life."* Although a person is saved by faith alone, faith is never alone, works of righteousness are to follow. (v20) The righteousness of the Christian has to exceed the righteousness of the super-strict and super-spiritual, law-abiding religious person and if not, you will by no means even enter the kingdom of God. Jesus said to the chief Pharisee, *'unless you are born again you cannot see the kingdom of God let alone enter.'* This should drive us to faith in Jesus and obedience to what He teaches, which exceeds all other forms of religious living and practice.

For John Wesley this was the key text of the Sermon of the Mount, in his discourse on this portion of Scripture in his sermons volume 5, he paraphrases the statement Jesus makes:-

I am come to establish it in its fullness, in spite of all the glosses of men: I am come to place in a full and clear view whatsoever was dark or obscure therein: *I am come to declare the true and full import of every part of it; to show the length and breadth, the entire extent, of every commandment contained therein, and the height and depth, the inconceivable purity and spirituality of it in all its branches.*

In these next six sayings of Jesus, He spells out what keeping the law really looks like and what He considers the main good works of Christian living:-

First, in relation to murder, *'you have heard that it was said to those of old, you shall not murder.'* This is the one thing people automatically appeal to when asking "are you going to heaven?" They answer, "I have not killed anyone, put a knife through anyone's heart or I am a vegan," they think it is more ethical or even spiritual because they are against killing of any creature. However, even these ethical principles will not be enough, for Jesus applies the outworking of this command to anger that is without any real cause. Anger can fill the human heart and the Christian is not immune to its damaging effects if not dealt with. The trouble is we don't get angry about the right things and often hold bitterness, grudges, resentment and malice. Holding on to these feelings can destroy and whoever does is in danger of hell fire, even if they claim to be a follower of Him.

(v23) God is more concerned that we live at peace with our brothers and sisters than the gifts we can use in worshiping Him. If you remember anyone has something against you, God's will for your life is to leave your gift on the altar and sort it out because it is not anger God wants but peace. This is an important lesson, although not easy to put into practice at times. Consider this, there is nothing worth coming before your relationship with God, God delights in those who worship Him in obedience and love. Remember, you are to be a peacemaker, so let your light shine.

Our righteousness is to excel in our relationships with others and also in the purity of heart. We are to be not only peacemakers but people of pure heart (Matthew 5:7-8 and 27-32). There is the issue of faithfulness and God loves faithfulness as it is one of the fruits of the Holy Spirit. God hates adultery and with God He does not just look on the outward appearance but He looks on the heart. The heart which is all important. Proverbs 4: 23 says *'keep your heart with all diligence for out of it spring the issues of life.'* David, after he committed adultery, prayed, *"create in me a clean heart O God, and renew a right spirit in me,"* Psalm 51.

What Jesus teaches here is far deeper in application than anything they would ever have heard and even today there is nothing like it, in all the schools of ethics and morality. The act, yes, is wrong but the thought, the lust and the sin of the eye, as human beings we are made to appreciate beauty and to acknowledge it. However, temptation begins often with what is pleasant to the eyes and a second look can spell trouble. In the words of Luther *'we cannot stop the birds flying over our head but we can stop them resting on our head.'* To dwell on such acts is to commit a heart sin, and we need to take this command to heart, when we consider how easy it is to access pornographic material through modern technology. This command covers all kinds of sexual impurity. Jesus could not be plainer on the subject, guard the heart.

The evangelical Church of today is failing with scandal after scandal but what is even more alarming is that the sexual agenda has high-jacked the Church. Things that are not even to be thought about are the topics of the day, discussed and even pandered to the desires of our fallen nature. We need to listen clearly to the drastic actions Jesus calls us to take. What He says is shocking and there is no way of watering down His words. If you think a relationship is good but it is a wrong one, pluck out your right eye, cut off your right hand. Listen to what Jesus has to say, *'it is better for you to do so than your whole body going into hell.'* If you are involved in such practice, the news is that you are not going to heaven, no matter what you think you believe, what you think about your spiritual life or the doctrines of grace you hold. Jesus can save you from a life of impurity but knows the dangers of those who live impure lives.

(v31-32) follows on because these Pharisees knew the law and one way out of adultery was simply to divorce and by giving a certificate of divorce, the Pharisees could usually have their cake and eat it. This was the thinking then and it is still the same today in some religious institutions. An example, in one section of the Church you cannot be a Priest if you have married a divorcee (v31) but if you are married, you can divorce your wife and remain a Priest, as along as the next wife you have has not been divorced - Hypocrisy! The disciples of Jesus are to have no part of it. Jesus wants His people to be lights, not only on the mission field, but bright lights in the family and in society, with a faithfulness and purity. A word to husbands, love your wives as Christ loved the Church and gave Himself for it.

(v33) Your righteousness is to be known in your speech and your speech is to be different even to the oath swearing religious community, which was a practice then as it is now. Swearing on that which is sacred (by God's temple and on the lives of others for example) should have no part for the Christian for two reasons; one, you have no power to promise anything (v36) then in your life people are to know you by your words, your 'yes is yes' and your 'no, no.' From your speech, people would learn that you belong to the truth because your life is true in word and deed. The best form of witness (even if you cannot preach) is speak the truth in all your words simply and straight, let your 'yes be yes' and your 'no, no.' This is a powerful witness, for you belong to Jesus who is the truth and the way and people need to see and hear this truth in our everyday lives.

(v38-39) Jesus says *"I tell you not to resist an evil person."* This is not referring to the abolishing of national armies so that nations cannot defend themselves against evil. These words are to be applied personally and it is not to do unto others as they do unto you. (v39) a slap is not a punch but rather a gesture which is an insult and if we are insulted then do not return the complement, let them carry on. Remember, Matthew 5:11 *'Blessed are you when they revile and persecute you, and say all kinds of evil against you' - great is your reward in heaven.*

If someone wants to take, give to them. How different is all this to the world? Whatever the outworking of these practical exhortations, there is a place in the Christian life where you will have gone the second mile when you did not have to. You would have given to someone who asked just to borrow from you and have not turned away. These are great challenges and you will face each of these in home, work, community and Church. Living in this world, be ready and prepared to be lights on a regular basis.

The last but not least of these, I say unto you, the Child of God is to extend love even to one's enemies, it does not mean you trust them but you love them. *'Bless those who curse you and pray for those who spitefully use you.'* Such people can be brought before God in their need. This is what is called unconditional love and it is the unconditional love of God that we have known in our lives through Jesus Christ, who went to the cross and laying down His life, although we could never deserve it. Jesus prayed for those who were doing the very killing, He prayed in love and not because they were good or great. God gives rain to both good and bad because it is His nature.

Look at the question in (v46) and think about it, *'If you love those who love you what reward have you?'* This section starts off in Matt 5:20 with the statement that your life is to be more righteous than the Pharisee but the fact is if we only love those who love us then we are no better than the tax collectors, because this is how sinners behave. The reality is this, no matter what we claim with our lips, our love is no better than that of sinners, who love those who love them. We have no place in the kingdom of God. Our righteousness is no better than the tax collector (v46) let alone the scribes and Pharisees!

(v48) is a tall order *'be perfect.'* This verse is the closing conclusion of this section and we have read in the first chapter that peacemakers will be called the *'sons of God'*. To live reconciled lives with our brothers and sisters is imperative for our relationship with God. There is purity of heart and if you have been born again of the Holy Spirit of God, you are people of the truth. In living at peace with people you are to trust in God and not to fight for your rights, turn the other cheek because you are the meek and you will inherit the earth. You are to love not only your neighbour but your enemies.

Not that we are perfect in any way but in the loving of those who are enemies, there is a perfection which is true righteousness. It is not that we are perfect and without sin but in all these areas of our relationship with others, purity in our relationships, truth on our lips, meekness in our spirit and love in our hearts, there is a completeness. Such living is a confirmation, a likeness to our Heavenly Father and so they will glorify your Father in heaven.

CHAPTER 3

DON'T BE LIKE THEM, DON'T BE SEEN

Matthew 6:1-18

1 'Take heed that you do not do your charitable deeds before men, to be seen by them. Otherwise you have no reward from your Father in heaven.

2 Therefore, when you do a charitable deed, do not sound a trumpet before you as the hypocrites do in the synagogues and in the streets, that they may have glory from men. Assuredly, I say to you, they have their reward.

3 But when you do a charitable deed, do not let your left hand know what your right hand is doing,

4 that your charitable deed may be in secret; and your Father who sees in secret will Himself reward you openly.

5 And when you pray, you shall not be like the hypocrites. For they love to pray standing in the synagogues and on the corners of the streets, that they may be seen by men. Assuredly, I say to you, they have their reward.

6 But you, when you pray, go into your room, and when you have shut your door, pray to your Father who *is* in the secret *place;* and your Father who sees in secret will reward you openly.

7 And when you pray, do not use vain repetitions as the heathen *do.* For they think that they will be heard for their many words.

8 Therefore do not be like them. For your Father knows the things you have need of before you ask Him.

9 In this manner, therefore, pray: Our Father in heaven, Hallowed be Your name.

10 Your kingdom come. Your will be done On earth as *it is* in heaven.

11 Give us this day our daily bread.

12 And forgive us our debts, As we forgive our debtors.

13 And do not lead us into temptation, But deliver us from the evil one. For Yours is the kingdom and the power and the glory forever. Amen.

14 For if you forgive men their trespasses, your heavenly Father will also forgive you.

15 But if you do not forgive men their trespasses, neither will your Father forgive your trespasses.

16 Moreover, when you fast, do not be like the hypocrites, with a sad countenance. For they disfigure their faces that they may appear to men to be fasting. Assuredly, I say to you, they have their reward.

17 But you, when you fast, anoint your head and wash your face,

18 so that you do not appear to men to be fasting, but to your Father who *is* in the secret *place;* and your Father who sees in secret will reward you openly."

It's impossible to convey the gripping attention this Sermon had on those who sat and heard Jesus speak. Every sentence is filled with power, meaning and relevance, beginning with a volley of *'blessed'* pronouncements concerning those who belong to the kingdom. Jesus speaks to those whose hearts have been humbled, who are willing to live by faith and take up their cross. They are told great things about themselves; you are the salt of the earth, a city set on a hill and the light of the world. These are staggering statements to make and we dare not apply them to ourselves unless the Lord has said so.

Jesus wants His disciples to shine brightly. Your parents wanted you to shine in school and Jesus bids us shine like a pure clear light. Jesus tells them their righteousness must exceed the most pious and that they are not to even look with lust. They should go the second mile and to have love, not only for their friends but also their enemies, otherwise it makes them no better than the tax collector.

In Matthew Chapter 6, Jesus sounds an alarm bell, a warning concerning their Christian life and walk. Jesus teaches about some dangers of life. He wants them to shine that the world may see their 'good works and glorify your Father in heaven.' *'But take heed, you do not do your charitable deeds before men to be seen by them!'* What? You're on the road, did you read the sign? I thought we were to shine, to be seen, now we are not? *Take heed* and listen carefully, you are on this path that your righteousness is to be better than scribes and Pharisees and there is a real danger to beware of - outward religion. If the devil cannot get you to veer off in the world, he will steer you into an outward form of piety as these things will be high on your agenda. You have become a religious person in a good sense but be careful there is danger.

The Christian's righteous deeds are not to be hidden but neither are they to be seen (v1-4). The Lord expects His disciples to do good works and to do charitable deeds. It is not 'if' but you 'will' be doing. You will be giving and showing acts of mercy, caring and doing good for the needy. These religious works of piety are mentioned first because they are the first in significance with true religion. Whatever else you think is important in your Christian life, James 1:27, pure and undefiled religion before God and the Father is this: to visit orphans and widows in their trouble. Two mistakes can be made, one is the neglect of such works and the other the way they are done. Jesus does not say that they are not to be done but rather not to be done so to be seen before others. Your good works are to be seen but they are not to be done to be seen. John Stott explains it like this: When Jesus tells them to shine it is because the temptation is to hide their light to other people, but when he says 'to hide' it is because the temptation is to shine – so the advice is 'where the temptation is to hide, you *shine* and where the temptation is to shine, you *hide*.'

Take heed then and be careful because such is the human heart we can turn good works into bad works. We can do acts of kindness not for the glory of God but for our own glory; not for the needs of others but to fulfil our own needs! It happens in all walks of life, not just political, or in the community but even in religious life and Christian work, it can be to the glory of ourselves. We are complex people but if this is the case then Jesus says we have our reward in full.

(v2) *"Therefore when you do a charitable deed do not sound a trumpet."* A trumpet is the instrument which draws attention, but there is no place for broadcasting 'making known' - blowing our own trumpet. I once saw a cheap plastic table, those white ones you use in the garden, given as a gift to a Church but what was worse, someone who shall be nameless, had placed a brass plaque on it with their name written on it - embarrassing!

(v3) Read carefully or it is all going to go wrong and you will end up wrong. The devil is good at what he does and can use even these words to take us to another extreme, what happens is we take measures in hiding our giving and deeds so that no one knows and in so doing we actually become more self-righteous in our actions. By taking action to hide what you are doing from others you become more fully aware of the good works you are doing . The problem is this, although no one else knows the works you have done, you do! Whereas, this verse tells us you are to do such works in such a way that you do not know yourself and you keep no record of your good deeds, *'don't let your left hand know what your right hand is doing.'*

We read an example of this at the end of time, in Mathew 25:38 *'When did we see you hungry?'* Those on that day had done good works but seem to have no knowledge of what they had done. Dietrich Bonhoeffer, in his work on the Sermon on the Mount, takes this to mean that the 'left hand does not know what the right hand is doing,' it is death to the old natural man and that it is what you are called to do, it is to live a crucified life (v4). Don't you blow the trumpet. If it happens, others see and they blow the trumpet, let that be the important thing these works are to glorify Him. You have to keep your eye on the ball; you need a singleness of eye on His glory. The important thing is the Father knows and keeps record. *'If you give someone a cup of cold water in the name of a Prophet, you will in no way lose your reward'* because you have not done it for men but for God. If you think that your works are of value only if they are seen, you're wrong. There is only one that sees and needs to see, you go and visit that elderly person who wouldn't remember the visit, no one has a clue, but there is another who sees all. As a nurse, a parent, a teacher, a neighbour, an employer or an employee, there are deeds that you do which only God sees and there is a great reward - the favour of the Father. This is all you need and is enough of a reward because it is the reward of the working out of His love.

Again, take heed that when you pray you will not be like the '*hypocrites*' and this word appears twice. What Jesus is saying is that in your Christian life you do not become actors. You are to do these things, but when you do them it is not for show. Jesus is not a fan of religious acting so be careful. There were those who loved to pray standing in the places of worship and on the street corners and they have their reward. The Lord is not against public prayer and to do so is a witness but to do it to be seen by others is a problem. One Minister said 'he had a member who would only come to Church if he was taking part and I worry about his salvation.'

(v6) *'Pray to your Father.'* Again, when you pray, the Lord wants you to pray and He taught His disciples to do so, more so than teaching them how to preach, prayer is of utmost importance. Whilst religion often may be concerned with the outward, the Lord is really concerned with the heart and what happens in the secret place. Here, is this great encouragement and instruction for your prayer life. There are three things that you need for prayer, a quiet place, a quiet hour and a quiet heart. We are to draw aside and shut the door from distractions. The Lord Himself practiced this, when He would go to a deserted place, but look all we need to know is this, your Father is in that place. He is waiting for you and it is an audience of only one and one prays, with eyes only for Him. Prayer is one of focus, speak to Him, think of Him, seek Him and your Father will reward you openly.

(v7) what not to do. There is such a thing as vain prayer and we all do it – stop! To quote Hamlet, *'Words without thought never reach heaven,'* it is not the fact that we just speak with our lips but often do not engage one's mind and heart or to pray in faith. Saying prayers, reading prayers, repeating phrases, we all do it and the cure is this, don't think that you will be heard for many words. This is not how prayer works, a few words and short prayers are often times better. Without faith it is impossible to please Him and He hears you not because of eloquence.

You have a Father who knows what you need yet it is very important to ask Him. This model prayer covers everything we need. You come to Him as *'Our Father.'* Prayer even in the secret place is a cooperative act. Our Father, give us this day… we come with the fellow children of God, we are to pray with others and for others also in mind, to a Father who is willing and able to hear. Pray like this: It contains six petitions, it contains everything that prayer should contain; worship, confession, petition, intercession and thanksgiving.

It can also be summed up with these words about knowing God, exulting God, obeying God and trusting God. The points: One is speaking to God the Father, who is in heaven. There is the spirit of adoption, the spirit of adoration, the spirit of submission, the spirit of supplication, the spirit of forgiveness and the spirit of godly fear. And then in one, almost footnote, that the

Lord brings out a vital truth concerning answers. We need forgiveness of sins and we also need a forgiving heart for others. There are also certain things that affect our prayers; one needs clean hands and a pure heart.

(v16) again, be careful for another religious duty that the disciple will be involved with is fasting. When you fast, not if, but the Lord definitely expected them to do so and gave them instruction on how they should engage with this practice. It is not the things of the world that are going to draw you away from the right path, it is religious duties which was the practice of the Pharisees and they fasted twice a week. It was also the practice of John the Baptist and his disciples, it is the practice of Muslims and all three of these acts are what Jews and Muslims and Christians are to be involved in: alms, giving prayer and fasting but the Christian is to do it differently.

Some deny its place believing our hungering should be spiritual not physical - blessed are those who hunger and thirst after righteousness. However, the Lord did fast in His perfect life and there are reasons for this practice.

John Stott highlights five in His commentary on the Sermon on the Mount:-

- It was the practice when there is a need to humble oneself before God, to deny oneself when suffering adversity and affliction, when God's favour was not with His people. The Anglican homilies call for this use when the blessing of the Lord was not with them (Matt 9:15).

- Also, when to seek blessing and power (Mark 9:29).
- Again, to venture out on a mission and when a special enterprise is to be undertaken. (Acts 13:3) *"Then having fasted and prayed and laid hands on them they sent them away."*
- Another reason is self-denial and self-discipline. As Christians we are called to beat our bodies, to run the race, to be in training as an athlete and the denial of bodily food, *"But in all things we commend ourselves as ministers of God"* (2 Corinthians 6:4-6). Furthermore, gluttony is a sin.
- Job 31:16, could say that *'if I have kept the poor from their desire, or caused the eyes of the widow to fail, or eaten my morsel by myself, so that the fatherless may not eat of it,'* a going without so others can eat.

Also, in (v16) we are instructed how to do so, 'do not disfigure your face and appear to be fasting.' There were those who noticed that Jesus and His disciples did not fast (Matt 9:14), yet it is quite clear Jesus taught them how. (v17) *'But you, when you fast, anoint your head and wash your face,'* for God is in the *'secret place'* with you and will *'reward you openly.'*

The Lord does not want you to pretend to be something you are not. The last hypocrite we want in the Church is one with a long face or the smiley face. Fasting is too be enjoyed and when you do it you will have more time to be in communion with the Lord. C.S. Lewis in Screwtape Letters, where older devil tells the younger apprentice, that they believed God to be a secret *'hedonist.'* He is a God of great joy. He is the blessed God and He wants His people to enjoy Him.

Now you are not to be like them in your motives. Don't do one's work to be seen, that is glory seeking for one's end and gain. You are to be different, not in the outward but in the inward. God sees the secret things and will bring every work into judgment, including everything, whether it is good or evil. There is a reward, a real reward and all that you have done is not unnoticed by Him. To God be all the praise, Amen.

Chapter 4

Wealth and Worry
Matthew 6:19-34

19 "Do not lay up for yourselves treasures on earth, where moth and rust destroy and where thieves break in and steal;

20 but lay up for yourselves treasures in heaven, where neither moth nor rust destroys and where thieves do not break in and steal.

21 For where your treasure is, there your heart will be also.

22 The lamp of the body is the eye. If therefore your eye is good, your whole body will be full of light.

23 But if your eye is bad, your whole body will be full of darkness. If therefore the light that is in you is darkness, how great *is* that darkness!

24 No one can serve two masters; for either he will hate the one and love the other, or else he will be loyal to the one and despise the other. You cannot serve God and mammon.

25 Therefore I say to you, do not worry about your life, what you will eat or what you will drink; nor about your body, what you will put on. Is not life more than food and the body more than clothing?

26 Look at the birds of the air, for they neither sow nor reap nor gather into barns; yet your heavenly Father feeds them.

Are you not of more value than they?

27 Which of you by worrying can add one cubit to his stature?

28 So why do you worry about clothing? Consider the lilies of the field, how they grow: they neither toil nor spin;

29 and yet I say to you that even Solomon in all his glory was not arrayed like one of these.

30 Now if God so clothes the grass of the field, which today is, and tomorrow is thrown into the oven, *will He* not much more *clothe* you, O you of little faith?

31 Therefore do not worry, saying, 'What shall we eat?' or 'What shall we drink?' or 'What shall we wear?'

32 For after all these things the Gentiles seek. For your heavenly Father knows that you need all these things.

33 But seek first the kingdom of God and His righteousness, and all these things shall be added to you.

34 Therefore do not worry about tomorrow, for tomorrow will worry about its own things. Sufficient for the day *is* its own trouble."

These words are as relevant and needful today as when Jesus spoke them and as human beings we are fundamentally no different from our ancestors. We have the same worries, problems and confronted with the same temptations and failings. Jesus touches on subjects that are of universal concern and common every day issues but which have spiritual and eternal consequence. In these verses we are confronted with two issues that people grapple with all over the world - religion and riches. The wisdom of Jesus Christ shines through not only in His miracles but in His teaching and it is perfect in choice, topics and balance. The natural, spiritual, practical teaching, simplicity and profundity of what is taught is astonishing. This is no rambling sermon and every arrow He takes to His bow strikes the mark.

Although the Lord is addressing His disciples, His words have a wider application, He wants them to be salt and light. Jesus wants them to be better and brighter than the religious and to have a righteousness that is not just outward but inward. *'Your righteousness should exceed the righteousness of the scribes and Pharisees'* (Matt 5:20). Now the Pharisees were not only interested in praise but also possessions – *'The Pharisees were lovers of money' (Luke 16:14)*. Religion, believe it or not, can be a way to riches, just look at the prosperity preachers of today. This is also an issue in the lives of His disciples, the plural, present, active, imperative - *'do not lay up'* (another translation - simply stop it)! Jesus has a lot to say about the issue of riches and on average one in twelve verses mentions it in the New Testament. Of all the subjects in proportion of words this is a major topic which Jesus touches on in His preaching to the crowds, and in the discipling of His followers. It is an issue that we have to deal with in the working out of one's faith.

The Lord is scratching were we all itch. There are certain things that God does not want you to do in life and this is one of them. Do not lay up treasures on earth because

He wants you to do something else, He wants you to lay them up in another place. Jesus does not want you to be poor but He wants you to be rich forever. Jesus wants the best for you in your life here on earth and in heaven, He wants you to live for those things which are everlasting.

Jesus teaches His disciples what to do with what they have by telling them not to lay up their treasures on earth. The person who does not know Christ only has this world and the things of this world to live for. The Christian, however, can know of other treasures which can be laid up in a place where they will not be destroyed. Jesus is the best financial adviser because He tells us where to invest and what to do with the possessions we have. Hear what He has to say and not what you think He is saying. Jesus is not against treasures but He wants you to think of what you do with them. Do not lay up for yourselves treasures on earth but rather invest in a safe place, in the kingdom of heaven. A good reason for this is that whatever you accumulate here on earth is going to be destroyed, moths will eat up those clothes you have in the wardrobe, your money will be eaten up with inflation and your car will rust away on the driveway. A fact of life, whatever is of this earth will not last and this is a scientific fact, not just a spiritual one. The Lord highlights this simple observable truth that whatever you are living for under the sun is not lasting.

Jesus is not against treasure but if you, in your life, can use what you have for the cause of His kingdom then you can actually invest your life for what will last forever. Sadly, even in Church life, we do not shine as lights because our thinking is darkened by the things of the world. This is witnessed sadly in Church life when members are more concerned by how little may be in the funds, when Jesus says you be careful when you have much in the Church funds and the laying up of riches in Church life is much more of a curse than a blessing. There is the real possibility that even as Christians our thinking can be darkened, our will affected and our love for Jesus Christ cannot burn so bright. Evidence for how bright our light is will be reflected so often in the Church finances. Jesus wants you to be light and we need to be not just to the world but to ourselves as a Church.

A Church which invests the resources they have into the things of God; the giving, the sharing, the venturing forth to reach out, to serve, to spread the word, the training up of Ministers, feeding the poor, holding services to support Missionaries, buying literature to cast seed, what they are doing is laying up treasures in heaven. However, things can go wrong and it is easy to take our eye off the ball. Think of the richest Church in the world with all of its wealth then ask the question is it blessed? How we long for the day when we could say with Peter and John to the lame man who sat at the temple gate in Acts 3:1-7, *'silver and gold have I none but what I have I give thee in the name of Jesus Christ of Nazareth raise up and walk.'* With all the wealth the Church holds onto, it is no longer able to say 'silver and gold have I none' but neither is it able to say to the one who is lame *'rise up and walk.'*

Remember, Jesus wants you to be the light and to shine. It is not that He does not want you to be rich here on earth but his main priority is that He wants you to be truly rich before God. However, living for these things can destroy our witness and our whole body can be filled with light or darkness in relation to the hold that things can have on our lives. Our relationship with material things can affect the heart. A word of caution here, there is no virtue in poverty or making yourself poor. Those who have been blessed with worldly goods have been a blessing to the cause of the kingdom of God in this world, with their support for the gospel but Jesus warns us that, *'where your treasure is there your heart will be also'* (v21). This will have an effect on the whole of your body, your heart, your, mind and your will.

Jesus speaks of a heart religion (v24). God is concerned with how riches can affect our spiritual lives. The lesson is that money is not the root of all evil but the 'love' of money is. If you live for this, this then is your treasure, and it is on earth, this is going to cause problems with spiritual sight because and we can become blind in this life. Remember, the Lord wants us to shine brightly and Jesus used an image of a lamp in Matt 5:15. The lamp of the body is the eye and how bright we are going to shine is to do with our eye and there is such a thing as the lust of the eye, the means by which sin entered into the world. Eve saw that the fruit was pleasant to the eyes. *If your eye is 'good' your whole body will be full of light,* the word for good, means clear, healthy.

We have read *'blessed are the pure in heart for they shall see God'* and this is what they are. The Authorised Version translates the word *'good'* as *'single'* (which is not a bad translation), stressing a fixed sight and a pure focus on the things of heaven and God. In the context of the chapter, the eyes of the hypocrites are not on God. They are doing religious works but they have an eye on man's applause and on being seen. They are looking and living for all things that are transient.

Many do not understand how living for the material riches can darken the soul and thinking. For example, those who do live for these things actually believe they are good and right and are showing great wisdom in this course of action. That is your light and if this light is darkness, how great is the darkness and this wisdom is brought into the Church. However, this line of thinking takes us off from God, from heaven onto what is transient. It spoils the Christian testimony and by doing so, we say to others these things are important and they are more important than Jesus and His kingdom.

Your heart can be bound, your mind, your will, and you will serve one and not the other. You are not free because you are governed by the pursuit of what you live for and

Jesus tells us we cannot serve both. Don't be like the ones who greatly distinguished themselves in life and in the last moments exclaim 'I have provided in the course of my life everything except for death, and now I am to die entirely unprepared.' It was Martin Luther, the Reformer, who said that when he had some wealth, he would give it away before it took hold of Him. It will cool your relationship with God so much so that you will not be able to serve Him. This has been the case with so many, even in Christian work, doing His work but not serving Him. If you are in business and God has blessed you with success, do what you do by serving God having your eye on heaven and what is lasting.

(v25) Therefore, because of the transient nature of things and because moral and spiritual vision can be distorted, He wants you to be free and you are to have unswerving allegiance, therefore, do not worry about these things. Jesus says not be over worried. See how relevant these subjects are. Things do not change because people still worry about what they have or what they do not have. The truth is the more you have the more you have to worry about.

We can worry about everything including life, money, home, family, children, the future, work, job prospects, promotion, health, and growing old. However, Jesus is not saying we should not be thoughtful because we know there are those around us who do not have any thought about the things of this life, who are totally irresponsible. Nevertheless, life is more than the body, there is also a soul and a spiritual realm. Life is more than all you see and God is the one who makes us wake up each day to enjoy that day. Life is more than a collection of biological components and more than just food or water, it has to do with God.

Jesus brings out three things His disciples need to know concerning God; His person, His provision and His providence. Jesus does not just say do not worry but the reasons why. It is no help telling people not to be so when their lives are falling apart, it can make matters worse (v26). Do not be anxious for God is Father of all, He is the creator and the source of all life. Someone put it like this, before they were a parent themselves, they believed that God would look after them but when they became a parent, they understood the truth more as they look after their children and they cannot forget them and they are mindful of them. Look at the smallest of God's creatures, the birds of the air and how we forget to look up and around us at this wonderful creation. God feeds them, He does not put the worms in their mouth but He has provided the food they need every day and they find it. Jesus reveals God as the heavenly Father, we forget this and we are his children and God then cares for us more than the birds of the air. Look up and stop being overly anxious because we cannot add anything to our lives. Worry takes away from life.

The provision of the flowers in the field is that they are alive today and then thrown into the fire. The fact is when we study them and look at their beauty *'even Solomon, in all of this glory was not arrayed like one of these, how much more does He clothe you (v30).'* He has clothed the flowers and they are thrown in the fire and how much more has He provided for His children for eternity greater garments than Solomon. As Christians He has provided us with the garments of salvation and He has clothed us with a robe of righteousness just as a bridegroom is arrayed. Matthew Henry gives this insight when he says 'let us not seek the glory of Solomon but rather his wisdom was out done by none but His glory was out done by the lilies of the field, knowledge and grace, are the perfection of man, not beauty, much less fine clothes, these lilies knew grace and so do we.'

(v31) Therefore do not worry about these three necessities although they are the basic needs of life. But when things become the main things in our lives to seek we become like the Gentiles. These are the people who do not know God and who have nothing else to seek in life. Remember you have a Father and the Father knows your need before you ask. Do not live like Gentiles who are taken up with the cares of the world, who live as if there were no God to care for them.

The disciples of Jesus are to live by faith, *'the just shall live by faith.'* If we do not remember all that Jesus has said from this chapter, (v33) is a verse to inscribe on our hearts. This captures the essence of the Christian's life in relation to the cares of life. Memory verses are not a bad thing. Try this one: *'Seek first the kingdom of God and His righteousness, and all these things shall be added unto you.'* Learn it off by heart as a Christian, and it will help us with decisions we have to make in life and remember, the kingdom of God comes first and never second.

There needs to be a singleness of eye which is on God, His course and His righteousness. However, our focus can be divided and our sight can become dark. We can live for a number of lesser things even as Christians, living for everything in the world, with a little bit for God. God says do not lay up treasures, not because He is against these things but get your priorities right and they will be added to you. So, therefore, do not worry about tomorrow and that is what you are doing in all the plans you're making, without seeking Him, because you have enough on your plate for today.

CHAPTER 5

THE IMPOSSIBLE POSSIBILITY
Matthew 7:1-12

1 "Judge not, that you be not judged.

2 For with what judgment you judge, you will be judged; and with the measure you use, it will be measured back to you.

3 And why do you look at the speck in your brother's eye, but do not consider the plank in your own eye?

4 Or how can you say to your brother, 'Let me remove the speck from your eye'; and look, a plank *is* in your own eye?

5 Hypocrite! First remove the plank from your own eye, and then you will see clearly to remove the speck from your brother's eye.

6 Do not give what is holy to the dogs; nor cast your pearls before swine, lest they trample them under their feet, and turn and tear you in pieces.

7 Ask, and it will be given to you; seek, and you will find; knock, and it will be opened to you.

8 For everyone who asks receives, and he who seeks finds, and to him who knocks it will be opened.

9 Or what man is there among you who, if his son asks for bread, will give him a stone?

10 Or if he asks for a fish, will he give him a serpent?

11 If you then, being evil, know how to give good gifts to your children, how much more will your Father who is in heaven give good things to those who ask Him!

12 Therefore, whatever you want men to do to you, do also to them, for this is the Law and the Prophets."

Jesus, in this Sermon gives great comfort to the anxious but also gives commands which drive us to our knees: to go the second mile, turn the other cheek, seek first the kingdom of God. Ultimately though, this Sermon is out to convict and convert, it turns our own thinking on its head. Our values, practices and lifestyles are to be superior to the most religious and different to tax collectors. If you think the Ten Commandments are hard to live by then the moral application Jesus makes in this Sermon simply brings us to our knees. In the words of Dr Martyn Lloyd-Jones *'I would rather make bricks without straw than try to live the Sermon on the Mount in my own strength.'* By the time we come to this final chapter of the Sermon on the Mount, the penny should have dropped that no-one is able to live such a life. What Jesus expects is way beyond anything we could ever humanly put into practice in our own strength. The life Jesus wants us to live is supernatural and He wants us to live it. Jesus is not speaking nonsense and you must believe that this is what He wants and expects. Because of Him, people have called this Sermon the 'impossible possibility.'

These verses (Matthew 7:1-12) begin with what we are not to do, then with what we need to do. Then finally what we need to do, summed up with the words in verse 12, *'Therefore, whatever you want men to do to you, do also to them, for this is the Law and the Prophets.'* This takes us back to the main body of the address (5:v17).

Let's begin with what may be the most quoted words in the Bible by non-Christians *'judge not.'* Having listened to the bulk of the Sermon and got this far, no matter how damning and convicting this Sermon may be, we can deflect the challenge with this thinking, 'I wish so and so could have heard this, it would have done them good.' What we have heard needs to be put into practice in our own life and what the Lord says speaks to me.

There is a fatal flaw in our fallen human thinking which is this – 'others are worse than we are' and we must put such thinking from us because it is wrong on so many levels. The most serious is that by judging others we take ourselves away from the mercy of God, which we ourselves need. We can have a self-righteousness in thinking that we are not like the Pharisee and in being different to the Gentiles and the tax collector we can become judgmental people. Jesus did not miss the mark with these words because He was speaking into a society, where certain sections of the community looked down on others, which was illustrated in the parable of the Pharisee and the Tax Collector.

The Pharisee goes up to pray and he thanks God that he is not like other men, unjust and unfaithful and he actually says *'not like this tax collector.'* He looks down on him and he judges himself better. Because of this he never knows what it is to be made right with God as he believes he is right, he never experiences mercy - he does not need it. It was this attitude of judging that placed these people *outside of the reach of Christ* – they came to him but always felt justified before him with their own righteousness. We must be careful of a judgemental attitude when condemning people with our own standards because the yard stick we use is crooked to begin with and we are in no position to do so. Jesus taught us by saying *'he who is without sin cast the first stone.'* However, we are making judgments that are wrong so much of the time. An example of this, if someone is considered poor, sadly in some Churches they are considered not worth bothering with. We have already read *'Blessed are the poor in spirit,'* while others may think we are wonderful and respectable we are actually not. We make judgments all the time and in life we are told what to do to be discerning (v15-16), *'by their fruits you will know them'* but writing people off, do not do.

The fact is we condemn people for doing those things we ourselves have often done. There are rules and values that we live by and we think that they are good and right but we do not keep them ourselves. We can be so merciless in our condemnation of others, but be careful because this is going to be measured back to you. We do not like it when people say unkind things about us but we have often said the same about others. We often make our judgements of others without thinking about the struggles and weakness they are going through. Take this instruction before you condemn your brother or sister for the speck in their eye by considering there may be a plank in one's own eye. It is incredible how we can be so blinded with our own faults – it is part of our human nature.

I heard a story of a Minister who had in the congregation a man who was in Hitler's SS and played his part in that terrible holocaust. He told the story that he was refused promotion in the SS because he was against dancing. Think of it, he was involved with killing thousands of Jews but dancing was a problem. This is an extreme example on this line of thinking. The problems is we get taken up with the outward when it should be the inward, the small things when it should be the big, by looking at other people's sins and not our own. What we need to do is to deal with the sins first. Good advice given in this statement is, be hard on oneself and lenient on others.

There is only one who has the right to judge, the Lord Jesus Christ and all judgment has been given into His hands. He knows everything there is to know about everyone, past, present and future. The inward thoughts and the outward actions, the pressures and temptations people bear and the weakness of our frame. His judgment is true, just and faithful and it is not that there is no judgment, but it is not for us to do so. However, modern society has taken these words to mean all kinds of sin are permissible, except intolerance, and we do not speak out to what is wrong. Nevertheless, the Bible makes it plain by stating that sin needs to be condemned and judgements are to be made.

Verse 6 is not about suspending our critical faculties. You, as His disciple, should be able to tell the value of a pearl and recognise pigs. We are to pray for the spiritual discernment we often lack. Things need to be judged:- teachings, practices, the spiritual claims people make, by reason, by conscience, by Scripture. *'Prove all things, and to hold fast that which is good.' The Apostle John exhorts us to* 'try the spirits whether they are of God,' but be careful not to take a position that God never gave us, so that we elevate ourselves thinking we are better, morally, spiritually, ethically and socially because such thinking can hinder our understanding of our own personal sin and need of grace. We need help, we need forgiveness, we need mercy, we need strength and we need wisdom for discernment, for knowledge, for new life.

So, it is in this context we read these words which in Luke's gospel is applied to prayer but in this context to our great need of these things, concerning salvation and the Christian life.

Ask for grace and help, the kingdom of God belongs to

the poor in spirit, those with needs and those who lack in the resources required. To come to the point of asking is a humbling experience because we are admitting we do not have and cannot do. However, with God there is the impossible possibility that His disciples could do what is asked of them by the Lord Jesus, what is impossible with man is possible with God. Jesus sees our spiritual need, if you are hungry and thirsty then ask for bread. In the words of the Heidelberg's Catechism, question 116, *'God will give His grace and Holy Spirit only to such as earnestly and without ceasing beg them from Him and render thanks unto Him for them.'* It has been said that if there are any regrets in heaven this will be one, how little we asked for the resources which were available to us. Jesus is not asking us but commanding His disciples to pray, with the encouragement that those who do will receive - seek and you will find. This is the second time in this Sermon where Jesus exhorts His disciples to seek (Matt 6:32). It is also the message of the Prophets of old, to seek God and it was this failure which brought spiritual harm to them. In the kingdom of God, the disciple needs to do two things; seek and find. This is what the kingdom of God is like (Matt 13:45). Nowadays, people seek happiness, relationship and meaning but they are lost at this step because they are seeking the wrong thing.

Jesus does not play games - knock and wait, then you can knock again. Do not beat down the door but just keep knocking and waiting. The Lord spoke of a woman who stood outside a house asking for bread at an inopportune time but she kept on knocking. In the state opening of parliament, the tradition is that Black Rod bangs on the doors of power three times and then the doors open. Jesus prayed three times and Paul prayed three times but the thorn was not removed, however, here we have a door that was opened after three knocks. The exhortation is to persevere and to be patient. Waiting is the hardest thing to do, so you keep on, you ask, you seek, you knock. In the Greek the tense is in the imperative, emphatic in the present, you keep on, you ask, you seek, you knock. We have a heavenly Father who knows your needs and He has not left you to the burden of your requests. Imagine if God gave you what you all asked for and gave it immediately, we would be in trouble. Remember, on many occasions we don't have the wisdom to know what is right to pray for, or even the fact that what is right may not be the best time to receive His gifts, but God does.

(v11) - He knows how to give good gifts. This refers to the spiritual benefits of the Gospel:-

Romans 10:15 - *'Who bring glad tidings of good things of the Gospel!'*

Hebrews 9:11 – *'Christ came as High Priest of the good things to come'.*

Luke 13:11-13 – In reference to the good things, for note when the article is present this refers to the Holy Spirit Himself, without the article it refers to the gifts of the Holy

Spirit. Jesus is instructing us to pray to this end for this divine love and power and strength.

Now the summation of all that Jesus has been teaching (Matt 5:17) *'do not think I came to destroy the Law or the Prophets.'* Therefore, whatever you want men to do, you (v12) show mercy, be forgiving, be righteous because you do not want others to judge you, you want them to be patient, kind and giving, this is what we want. This must be the only place in Scripture where we are instructed to think of ourselves first but in so doing think and learn what you are to do unto them. This is the Law and the Prophets and perhaps this must be the second most quoted verse of the Bible, by those who don't believe the Bible, or those who don't read it. The most quoted, the least preached and even less practiced! To be honest, we don't know what to do with the teaching of this verse and we may even be a bit frightened of it or shy away from it as gospel believers. It's often skipped over in commentaries or ignored and we don't know how it should be applied or how it fits into our theology. The focus seems too man-ward and not God-ward and it seems to be speaking of works rather than grace. It is practical but not doctrinal and at the end of the day, it is an ideal and not real!

Let's look at it from the angle of Jesus Christ who teaches us this first. We see in this verse in the mind and the heart of the Lord Jesus that He came to fulfil God's law. He speaks of God's law and teaches it, He loved it, lived it and in the end lay down His life for others with such love and fulfilled all that the law required. This is imperative, it is not a suggestion or something to be discussed, it is something to be done and Jesus filled it perfectly. In His perfect life He commands us to do the same, although imperfectly. Therefore, this verse is in connection to all that is spoken of in seeking, asking and wanting to know the good gifts of God, so that you can do unto others as you would have them do to you. There is the vertical dimension on calling on God, asking so that we may engage in the horizontal living with others.

It is all very practical, when you walk down the street you would rather your neighbour say *'hello'* and greet you than pass you by. You would also like someone to show appreciation or thanks if you did something for them. Be on time in your appointments and if not, let them know if you cannot, you want people to be honest and truthful with you and you want someone to give a helping hand when you are struggling. You want to do the same to them not because you are just thinking of yourself but because you are thinking of God and His law and Glory.

This carries us beyond the love of sentiment to the love that is seen in action. It is useless to feel kindly to others if we do not act fairly yourself. It covers 'all things whatsoever'. It applies generally not merely to brethren, friends, neighbours, fellow-Christians and fellow-citizens. It also applies to strangers, disagreeable people, foreign people and the non-Christians. This verse is a clear guiding light of how we can best perceive what we should be like and we know how we should like to be treated under certain circumstances. Accordingly, we may see how others would also wish to be treated. This is reasonable and there is nothing unfair in what is laid upon us. No-one can possibly complain of this rule because it is a principle of perfect justice and everyone is to be his own judge in regard to it. What we most desire we should be ready to give to others, *what we greatly enjoy we should be ready to share with others: What we have received we want others to possess.* 'Love seeks not her own.'

CHAPTER 6

BEWARE, BE NOT DECEIVED, BE WISE

Matthew 7:13-29

13 "Enter by the narrow gate; for wide *is* the gate and broad *is* the way that leads to destruction, and there are many who go in by it.

14 Because narrow *is* the gate and difficult *is* the way which leads to life, and there are few who find it.

15 Beware of false prophets, who come to you in sheep's clothing, but inwardly they are ravenous wolves.

16 You will know them by their fruits. Do men gather grapes from thornbushes or figs from thistles?

17 Even so, every good tree bears good fruit, but a bad tree bears bad fruit.

18 A good tree cannot bear bad fruit, nor *can* a bad tree bear good fruit.

19 Every tree that does not bear good fruit is cut down and thrown into the fire.

20 Therefore by their fruits you will know them.

21 Not everyone who says to Me, 'Lord, Lord,' shall enter the kingdom of heaven, but he who does the will of My Father in heaven.

22 Many will say to Me in that day, 'Lord, Lord, have we not prophesied in Your name, cast out demons in Your name, and done many wonders in Your name?'

23 And then I will declare to them, 'I never knew you; depart from Me, you who practice lawlessness!'

24 Therefore whoever hears these sayings of Mine, and does them, I will liken him to a wise man who built his house on the rock:

25 and the rain descended, the floods came, and the winds blew and beat on that house; and it did not fall, for it was founded on the rock.

26 But everyone who hears these sayings of Mine, and does not do them, will be like a foolish man who built his house on the sand:

27 and the rain descended, the floods came, and the winds blew and beat on that house; and it fell. And great was its fall."

28 And so it was, when Jesus had ended these sayings, that the people were astonished at His teaching,

29 for He taught them as one having authority, and not as the scribes."

We began this series by saying the teaching of Jesus reveals His glory as much as His miracles do. His wisdom, love, righteousness and authority shine through. Jesus said He is the fulfilment of the Law and the Prophets who came to die for our sins and bring people back to God. However, before Jesus went to the cross He preached, calling people to repent for the kingdom of heaven is at hand. At the heart of this Sermon is the cross, it is searching and convicting as well as comforting, challenging and converting. No-one spoke like Jesus, there was not just a glory about His words and in this last section we catch an urgency of what He was teaching. The stakes could not be higher. He did not come saying this world is a friendly place for the follower of Jesus. This is a heartfelt appeal that the Lord makes to those who are before Him, to be careful and to be wise.

The Lord speaks these closing words in the most urgent and simplest of appeals, asking them to act upon what they have heard. *'Enter by the narrow gate'* is a real appeal that Jesus makes to all those who have been listening. Once you have been confronted with the words of the Lord Jesus Christ, you stand at the cross-roads of life. There is a narrow gate that Jesus wants you to enter and a broad gate He wants you to avoid, because one gate leads to life and one leads to destruction. He is the God of life and He wants you to live. This, however, is not an easy step to take as it is a narrow gate and don't even begin to believe that there are many ways to God and all roads lead home, as it is not the teaching of the Bible and of the Lord Jesus Christ. There is only one way to heaven and that is through Him alone. It is a difficult path taking up the cross because there is going to be persecution, turning the other cheek and even losing life and limb but it is also about seeking treasure in heaven. As the children's chorus goes:- *There's a way back to God from the dark paths of sin; there's a door that is open and you may go in. At*

Calvary's cross is where you begin, when you come as a sinner to Jesus. You have to humble yourself as a big head will not fit through this narrow gate.

The way is so narrow that you would almost miss it as you go through life and the majority of people are heading for the broad gate. The way is broad with many other religions and belief systems you could try, which may be more appealing, but this way is slower because it is filled with danger and it is difficult. When you come to this gate it can only take one at a time, you have to enter it alone and then you have to humble yourself and then when you do, it is so narrow you cannot carry anything with you. Those things that you hold onto are to be left behind, including one's own good works but the stakes could not be higher, you need to find it and you need then having found it - to enter. The narrow gate goes against the flow because the natural instinct is to go with the flow and this gate can be lonely, slow and difficult.

John Favel, a Puritan lists 12 paths that can lead to Hell:

1) Children denied Biblical teaching by their parents.

2) Ignorance about Christ.

3) Worldliness.

4) Sinful habits.

5) The love of sensual pleasure.

6) The cares of the world.

7) Groundless presumption.

8) Formal religion.

9) Profanity.

10) Debauchery.

11) Prejudice against Christianity.

12) Hypocrisy and reliance upon respectability.

There are only a few who find the gate, many *try to find it,* many who know about it and many who think they have found it but they are on the wrong path because they are going in the wrong direction. Jesus exhorts them in (Luke 13:24) - strive to enter it.

Make sure you have come to Jesus, leave all and put your trust in Him, be obedient and follow, although everything is against you. The gate is not easy to find, time is short and many are far off the right path. Also, they do not have the strength of heart and mind for such a journey. Many have come to the gate only to find that they could not rid themselves of all that they had gathered in this world and would not leave their possessions behind for the next. Then they realise this is not a quick, easy step, the path is difficult. Walk carefully, thoughtfully and patiently as it is not easy but it leads to life and the Lord wants you to find life. He came into this world to save people from going to hell and He stands with His arms open wide with His love, urging you to come to the gate which is difficult to find.

The preaching of Jesus was so different to that of the scribes and the preaching of today, where the preacher speaks with hands in their pockets, are laid back, cool and funny but there is no pointing to the right way and there is no warning of destruction, and like the scribes in many ways exegetically right but ethically devoid of any reality of the gospel of Jesus Christ. It was Spurgeon who said 'if people want to go to hell then they have a free choice to do so. But they will have to do so walking over my body, going against my tears, appeals and you are free to do so but it will be over my bended knees and prayers.' This Sermon of Jesus is not just interesting, it is essential, it is urgent and it is an appeal to be saved.

There is more, you are being exhorted and you are being warned. Also, the Lord wants you to find life but there is another who does not want you to find this path because in this world there are false Prophets who come in the name of God and many people are taken away from the gate. When Jesus is speaking of the narrow and broad way, this can be applied to false teachers who are speaking about religion and Christ but they themselves have not entered in. There is much confusion and hindrance on the path to Jesus. Jesus is the great Prophet and what He has said in this Sermon has come true in every generation, false Prophets have come to His people, His flock, His little lambs and they will come to you.

Jesus closes with these words of warning, beware, no matter how few or small and insignificant God's people may be, ravenous wolves will come to destroy. In every letter of the New Testament you will find reference to those who try and pass themselves off as belonging to Christ but they do not. They pretend they are from God but come with fake news, so beware because there is not a Church or a Christian who will have the luxury of being spared from this attack. They come in disguise and look like sheep. Sheep and wolves are two different creatures, one is harmless and the other seeks to devour. When such people come into the Church denying the central elements of the faith, like the blood of Christ, salvation, the denial of the Bible being the Word of God, salvation by faith alone. When these people come to you, they are wolves in wolves' clothing but Jesus is speaking of wolves in sheep's clothing. They use the evangelical jargon, they say their prayers and do Christian works but watch out as they are not so easy to spot, so every Christian needs to be on guard. For narrow is the way, it is not worldliness so often but brands of Christianity which can take you from Christ. If someone says to you enjoy the world, you will not be taken in but the super pious with great claims of spiritual experiences can make you gravitate towards such people. Beware, be careful, be discerning and don't think it cannot happen to you.

(v20) - *'Therefore by their fruits you will know them.'* The true Christian should be possessed with some spiritual critical faculties and be able to discern, to some measure, those who are from God or not (1 John 2:27). Consider the words in the beginning of this chapter, *'Judge not, that you be not judged,'* this does not mean that the Christian is just to believe everything that a person says, you are to have knowledge and understanding and discernment, these are spiritual gifts. One of the marks of a Christian is that they would not be deceived, *'if it were possible to deceive even the elect'* and this has nothing whatsoever to do with intelligence but spiritual understanding. The unbiblical claims TV evangelists make are often utterly unbiblical and outrageous. Some can watch it instead of the comedy channel but the tragedy is that many are taken in and it leads from the narrow gate.

One of the ways to discern this is to look at their lives. By the fruits you will know them, look at what they produce not what they profess, it is not words. J. C. Ryle said 'sound doctrine and holy living go together and what one believes will affect one's behaviour.' Ask the question 'is one's life in accordance with the teaching of the Lord?' Not words, some people have a lot of leaves, but not good fruit. (v19) The Christian bears good fruit but with these it is not that they produce no fruit it is that of bad fruit, it is not love to God, faith in Christ, repentance, confession and obedience.

Be warned though, not everyone who calls me Lord will enter the kingdom of heaven. Having respect for Jesus will not be enough. One may make a confession *'whoever calls upon the name of the Lord shall be saved.'* Neither is it what we do. There are some wonderful people and they do good works so they must be Christians? However, being a preacher and teacher is no guarantee. Those Ministers who claim their great gifts of healing is no guarantee, even though they are great miracle workers. One can have a great enthusiasm 'Lord, Lord' and say it with great gusto, rather it is those who do the will of the Father, shall enter the kingdom of God.

People can go a long way in religion proclaiming they are Christians by making great statements, doing good works, undertaking Christian service, obtaining remarkable success in their work and being noted for their practical energy and miracles. They were diligently orthodox, do everything in the name of Christ and do so to the end, but no-one enters heaven by what they *'do'*. They did all these things but it was not the will of the Father. There can be faith in miracles but no justifying faith, gifts of tongues but no real holiness. Working miracles without grace will never bring a person to heaven. They practise lawlessness and the broad road is lawlessness. Martin Luther said he 'would rather do one work of obedience than a miracle.' The Church knows you, the world knows you, but does Jesus know you?

So, there are two ways, two trees, two claims and there are two ends. Jesus tells us here of two responses to this Sermon. (24-27) Like builders, one builds a house and it stands, the other builds a house and it falls. The response from the people was that they were astonished at His doctrine and they marvelled at it. Jesus is different to all religious teachers, he is different from the other religious leaders of the day who had position and place above the people, Jesus was endued with the power of authority. He towers over all the great teachers of this world. Sir Edward Arnold, one of the greatest authorities on Buddhism, declared that *'one sentence from the Sermon on the Mount was worth more than Buddha had ever taught.'*

Now look at the different responses to the Sermon, one was a doer of the word. The house which stood was built by the builder who put Jesus' words into practise. He lived his life in accordance with the word of Jesus and was a builder who took the plans which were laid down by the architect and followed them. This person is the one who follows the plan of Christ that He has laid down, if a builder does not, it will not be long before the builder is in trouble.

This is not the case with the builder who knows better. We may see that from time to time, a builder will come along who never needs the plans, because they think they know it all. These people listen to the words of God yet still they know better. The contrast that Jesus makes of these two builders is that one is wise and the other is foolish.

The end of the Sermon is this, *'everyone who hears these sayings of mine, and does not do them will be like a foolish man who built his house on the sand and the floods came, and the wind blew beat on that house and it fell, and great was it's fall'* - these final words were ringing in their ears because there are storms that we all have to face. The wise person and the foolish person have to face the fact that there is no dispensation for anyone. All the storms in our lives are nothing compared to what we will one day have to face. We go through life and it does not take long before the rain begins to descend upon us and we learn from an early age of illness, weakness and frailty. There is no escape for these are the words of the Lord Jesus Christ and there is no other conclusion.

And after all was said, you could hear a pin drop as the house fell and the people were astonished at His teaching.

SUMMARY

Over the years, we at Bethesda Chapel have gone through our Lord's teaching on many occasions. It is a thrilling proclamation of what it is to be a Christian and the life of a true believer. Jesus Christ fills the eyes of those who belong to Him with a vision of what God's kingdom on earth should be like, fills the heart with a purpose and a way of life far beyond anything we as human mortals in the history of the world have ever risen to. Jesus inspires the soul of His people to better and higher things of Christian living, which when thinking about again excites and challenges the whole of one's being to praise which says, 'thank you Lord for such a life,' although there is not a natural atom in me which could ever live such a moment, yet this is Your plan and Your desire and Your will and it is good.

The hope is that this little booklet will be a means to focus once again on what the Lord Jesus taught concerning the Christian life and how dynamic and radical the Christian life is compared to how the Christian life is outworked after 2,000 years of tradition. The understanding of this message of Jesus is a 'must' for a follower of Jesus. Sadly, in the history of the Church much has been added to the Christian faith and practice which not only has little correspondence but often a direct contradiction to what the Lord taught. How can this be? How do people come to the idea that this message is directed to the social order of society, when the people Jesus is speaking to are those who come to Him after firstly belonging to the kingdom of heaven? Blessed are the poor in Spirit, how can one reading the Lord's teaching on being salt and light believe that spiritual Christian living is to be practiced by cutting oneself off from the world? How can one reading the claims that Jesus makes concerning Himself being the fulfilment of the law come to the idea that a Christian needs to go back to a life of law fulfilment? How does one come to the idea in reading the requirements needed to enter the kingdom of heaven think they can honestly are able to do so? How is it that when Jesus deals with the things in the kingdom which really matter such as anger, lust, speaking truthfully, giving and loving enemies, a Christian is pleased to take up with the outward workings of ritual religion? How can a Christian come to believe that just speaking and knowing about Christian things is a complete Christian life, when Jesus obviously expects His disciples to be involved with deeds of charity? How has the Church ended up praying so little when Jesus gives such encouragement and instruction to this end? How is it that when reading this Sermon, a Christian does not know the importance of the need to be forgiven and forgiving? How is it that the gospel of health and wealth is even tolerated as a teaching in the Church, when the Lord warns against laying up treasures on earth and not to worry about tomorrow? How is it that after all that is said, someone comes to the idea and thought that this life which Jesus speaks of can be lived without the desperate need of the grace of God?

The reason for these questions is the miss-applying of the Sermon. Some take its words to apply to society as a whole and some interpret it to apply only to the Jews of Jesus' day who generally did not heed the call concerning the kingdom of heaven, but will (according to this understanding) apply as the constitution for the millennium kingdom of the future. In short, it does not apply to New Testament Christians who believe and live between the period of Christ's first coming to His second coming. It may have some principles to teach and to draw out but this Sermon simply is not the blue print of those who are living under the dispensation of grace so they say.

One reason for this idea is that this Sermon misses many elements of New Testament teaching connected with the gospel of Christ, such as the need for faith and to believe. There is no mention of the cross or the need of sacrifice and the blood, new birth, grace or teaching concerning the doctrines of the cross such as justification, no atonement or teaching concerning the person of Jesus

Christ Himself. So the conclusion is that this Sermon is not for New Testament Church believers.

However, this study has taken the line of thinking that everything mentioned above is present in this Sermon, such as new birth, grace, faith, the cross, sacrifice, the unconditional love of God and righteousness, the person and work of Jesus Christ. All these things are woven into the very fabric of the whole address and it would be an impossible task to separate this gospel's realities from the Sermon. This message is addressed primarily to those who have come to Jesus Christ and to those who have learned about Him, or who are beginning to learn and follow Him, who feel the authority of His claims, the attractiveness of His being and who are being called or allured to the belief in the Saviour. Jesus is speaking to those who know they have been blessed. It is the most foundational understanding that the person who comes to Jesus Christ knows the blessing of God upon them and they stand as those who are no longer under the curse but under the favour of God. They are people who know of great need, are poor in spirit, have a hunger for righteousness, know of mercy and have a heart which is pure and clean. We are speaking here of what the Prophets spoke about when they referred to those who, under the New Covenant, had a heart of flesh.

What all true Christians agree on is it's not only the right understanding of the Sermon but it needs to be lived out by lives which have radically been changed by the person and power of Jesus Christ and no matter how long you have been a Christian these Bible chapters challenge, thrill, comfort, convict and call the Christian ever upward.

The blessing of God's word is always in the application, '*be a doer of the word.*' These are words we need to know. They are words of Salvation, the hearing and the doing of them has eternal significance for the soul who comes to believe in Him and trust Him as Lord and Saviour. But hearing them is not enough, studying them is not enough, they have to be applied into the heart and life.

'*All Scripture is given by inspiration of God, and is profitable for doctrine, for reproof, for correction, for instruction in righteousness, that the man of God may be complete, thoroughly equipped for every good work*'(2 Timothy 3:16-17). However, it is true to say that there are certain portions which are more helpful and useful than others, '*man cannot live by bread alone but by every word which proceeds from the mouth of God.*' There are portions of Scripture where the gold gems lay on the surface and need little digging to understand what is being said and such is the Lord's Sermon on the Mount. The main problem the reader will find with this Sermon is not the understanding of what is said but rather the application of what the Lord teaches.

The mistake some make in its application is believing that what is taught in this Sermon relates to all people and there is no doubt that the words of Jesus have something to say to all people of every age. However, when the Lord spoke these words it was firstly to His disciples who were gathered around Him and those who had come to follow Him. There is something being taught us by the Lord in this Sermon of the impossible possibility of Christian living.

To try and apply what the Lord's teaching to those who do not come and believe in Him is never going to work. So, if anyone says they value the ethical teaching found in this Sermon and would like it to be applied and worked out more in the world, then they need to come to Jesus Christ by faith and accept Him as Lord and Saviour, for without which this Sermon has nothing whatsoever to say to them in their lives than the need to be saved.

If you ever find that Church life is hard, disappointments come, or the road has been filled with the wrong teaching or practices which just suck out the power of the Christian life, this is a portion to come back to time and time again. Learn what the Lord's vision for your life is to be and you will find holy passions being revived and zeal being infused once again in your soul, prayer will flow and grace will come to you.

Read as much as you can on the teaching concerning the Sermon on the Mount and let it be one of the constant themes of study in your Christian life. It will save you from a form of Christianity which is word only and without power, it will save you from a dead orthodoxy which does not even thrill you. It will save you from a form of Christianity which separates you from Jesus Christ, the Saviour Himself. It will even save you from the brand of religion which is taken up with a doing and activism rather than teaches us of the importance of communion and our relationship with God the Heavenly Father.

May God give you, not only understanding, but the will and power to then put into practice this which pleases Him, so that your light will shine before men, that they may glorify your Father in heaven.